Wiccan Holiday Cookbook

Dawn Flowers

Other Books by Dawn Flowers

The Book of Dark & Light Shadows

The Spell Book of Wiccan Shadows: Over 200 Wiccan Spells

Witch Wars: A Witches Combat Manual

Help with Hauntings:
A Guide to Cleansing your Home of Spirits and Ghosts

Book of Cleansings: The Professional's Prayer Book

Coming Back Soon!
The Little Wiccan Learning Series, Volume 1: Book of Magic
The Little Wiccan Learning Series, Volume 2: Activity Book
The Little Wiccan Learning Series, Volume 3: Book of Shadows

Table of Contents

DRINKS..9

APPETIZERS...33

MAIN COURSES..57

DESERTS..69

Merry Meet!

Within this book you will find a variety of meals to suit any event. There are drinks for hot days or freezing nights, meals for two or twenty, and dishes that are appropriate for any Wiccan gathering, day or night.

Because many of us these days simply don't have the time to roll out dough from scratch to make an old style pie, I have tried to include recipes within this book that are practical to our busy lifestyles. Most people have jobs outside the house and come home to find children running around demanding our attention. I understand this, and I too live this lifestyle as well. I wish we had time to sit around and peel apples for a pie, or shell peas for a stew, but we all have other demands. Despite our busy lifestyles, the old-time techniques for cooking do not have to be completely thrown out the window. You can still make a homemade apple pie without spending hours peeling apples and rolling dough. Today, we can buy pre-made dough, and even pre-peeled apples in a ready to bake sauce. OK, I know, if we use these ingredients, it sounds unlikely that we will end up with a traditional, home-style apple pie like our Great Grandmothers used to make, but you can! Using modern ingredients to make cooking more convenient doesn't have to mean that we sacrifice flavor and appeal to save time in the kitchen. For example, let's say that we use a pre-made pie crust along with pre-made apple pie filling: If that's all you use, then your pie might come out tasting rather bland, nothing like an old-style pie. But, if you add a little sugar and spice here, with a pat of butter there, and a little something over here, then BAM, you've got yourself a dang delicious pie that will be the envy of your friends. If you throw away all of the wrappers and cans you used in your pie, no one would ever be able to tell the difference, and it could be your little secret that everything wasn't completely from scratch.

Within this book, I will not pretend that I am a great chef, but I will admit that I can cook a few tasty dishes and keep people fed with foods they like. Many of the recipes within this book are ones that have been passed on to me by my Mother and Grandmother. Several recipes are ones that I managed to come up with on my own, in the hopes of recreating something I had previously eaten and thought tasty. Other recipes are ones that I found in books, and modified to make them suit my family's palate. Some recipes I found in books, and left them alone because they were perfect in their original form. Before each recipe in this book, I will try to give a short history of the recipe, such as where I found it, or who gave it to me, or what I changed from the original recipe, and I will certainly give credit where credit is due, although I have had most of these recipe for years, and simply do not remember where many of them came from.

I have presented these recipes in the common format of categorizing them by dish type, however, towards the end of the book I have created sample menus for various holidays and events which might prove useful to help you plan for a party or gathering.

I hope you and your family and friends enjoy these delights as my own family and friends have, and I encourage you to substitute ingredients, add some spices, and do what you can to make them your own. At the end of every recipe I have provided space for you to add your personal notes for future reference.

Merry Part & Bon Appetite!
Dawn Flowers

Drinks

Spiced Cider Wine

This is one of my most popular refreshments, especially on cold evenings. This tasty hot toddy is sure to keep your guests warm and fuzzy.

When visiting the Renaissance Festival several years ago, my husband ordered me a drink that I found absolutely delicious. This recipe is a recreation of that drink, and it comes pretty darn close! Our friends just love it, and beg for it every year.

Ingredients
16 packages of Spiced Cider Mix
1 Gallon of White Wine

Optional Additions:
5 Cinnamon Sticks
5 Clove Pieces
½ Cup Sugar

Preparation:
Pour the wine into a large pot, and warm over medium heat. When the wine begins to become hot, add the packages of Spiced Cider Mix and stir until the wine becomes clear again. This will only takes a few minutes. (NOTE: You may want to add 10 packages first and do a taste test, and then add one package at a time until you get the desired taste. If you get the wine too strong with the mix, don't worry - just add more wine.) 16 packages usually work best, but it may vary depending on the brand of spice mix that you use. If you choose to add the sugar, cinnamon sticks, and/or cloves, do this after you have added the packaged spice mix.

Serving Suggestions:
This recipe is supposed to serve 16 people; however, most people come back for more, several times, so it really only serves 5-10, depending on how tipsy people are willing to get. When I prepare Spiced

Cider Wine, I usually leave it in a large pot on the stove and keep it on the lowest warm setting. I leave a large ladle with mugs nearby. Throwing in a couple of cinnamon sticks adds a little bit of flavor, and will also look nice if you have guests serve themselves. Some people may find this drink a bit tart (if they are not used to drinking wine) so adding about a half a cup of sugar can help make it a little smoother and sweeter of course. This drink is also fun and easy enough to prepare outside in a cauldron over a fire. This dish is best served warm, so putting it into a punch bowl may not be a good idea because it will begin to cool quickly.

Caramel Apple Cider
Non-Alcoholic

This refreshment is another drink that keeps you warm during those long winter nights, and its non-alcoholic, so the little ones can enjoy it too. I ordered a similar drink at a Starbucks one evening, and the next day I rushed to the store in search of ingredients to make my own. My husband says this recipe is much better than what you get at the store, so I hope you enjoy it too. The recipe below is for one individual drink, but you can make it for a larger group by using the conversion table at the back of the book.

Ingredients
1 Cup Apple Juice (Or Apple Cider)
2 Teaspoons Caramel Syrup
1-3 Large Spoonfuls of Cool-Whip®
    Whipped Cream

Preparation:
Pour the apple juice into a mug and add the caramel syrup. Put the drink into the microwave until it is warm (depending on your microwave, this may take 30 seconds to a minute and a half.) Once the drink is warm, stir it well, then top it off with whipped cream and it is ready to serve.

Serving Suggestions:
Because this drink should be served immediately, (or else the whipped cream will melt and it will lose its beautiful appearance) I make this drink one at a time as guests want them. Also, when purchasing the caramel syrup, you should not get actual caramel, nor should you use caramel topping like you would put on ice cream, but rather, you need to use caramel syrup like you would put into a coffee drink. Otherwise, it will not mix well and will be clumpy.

Witches Brew Ha

This brew is sure to make any party more festive. This is a powerful brew, sure to make you loose your broom, so hold on tight! This is a variation of the popular trashcan punch.

Ingredients
1 Gallon Everclear®
3 dozen small pieces of assorted fruit & melons
8 liters of Lemon Lime Soda (Sprite® is great)
1 - 5th Fruit Schnapps
1 - 5th Vodka
1 - 5th Rum
1 - 5th Fruit Brandy
1 package Powdered Tropical Punch Kool-Aid® mix.

Preparation:
The night before you want the brew ready, take the fruit pieces and soak them in the gallon of Everclear®. The next day, add all of the other ingredients and stir.

Serving Suggestions:
The fruit that you use in this punch can be your preference. From experience, I can recommend watermelon, strawberries, grapes, orange slices, cantaloupes, pineapples, lemons, limes, and honey dew melons.

You can also encourage guests to bring their own favorite fruits or liquor to add to the can. After a few drinks of this brew, you won't care what they add!

Bitchin' Beltane Brew

This is another great Witches brew to get any party going strong and it will keep the guests flying high!

Ingredients
2 Parts Orange Juice
1 Part 7-Up®
1 Part Peach Schnapps
1 Part Sour Mix
1 Part Whiskey
1 Splash of Grenadine

Preparation:
Mix all of the ingredients together and add ice to the bowl or pitcher and serve. It's a very simple recipe with no night before preparations needed, which makes it a great punch to serve on the spur of the moment.

Serving Suggestions:
Serve this drink cold over ice and garnish with a small orange slice.

Skyclad Punch

This recipe is great for cooling down during those hot Lughnassad festivities in August. It's easy to fix and will have you feeling fine in no time. Just try and remember where you put your clothes after you've had a few glasses of this Skyclad Punch!

Ingredients
1 Liter of Vodka
9 Quarts Beer
16 oz. Frozen Concentrated Lemonade
1 Bag of Ice

Preparation:
Mix together the Vodka, Beer, and Lemonade, then add the bag of ice and stir once more to blend.

Southern Sweet Tea
Non-Alcoholic

I have lived in Texas my entire life, and our hot summers demand a lot of ice cold drinks, and Southern sweet tea is a favorite in my neck of the woods.

Ingredients
1 Gallon of Water
1 ¼ Cup Sugar
3 Family Sized Orange Pekoe Black Tea Bags
   (Lipton® or Luzianne® would be fine)

Optional Additions:
Mint Leaves
Lemon Slices
Peach Extract

Preparation:

There are two ways you can effectively prepare this southern favorite. The first is known as Sun Tea. Place the water and the tea bags into a glass jug and let it sit in the sun for several hours. When the tea has become dark, you can add the sugar and stir until it is clear.

The second method is much quicker, and happens to be the one I use most, since I make tea almost daily. In the pitcher or jug, add two cups of very hot water. Add the sugar and stir until the water runs clear. Now add the tea bags and stir gently and slowly, so as not to tear the tea bags. When the water becomes dark (after about a minute or two) you can now add the rest of the water to the jug or pitcher. If you want your tea to be cold in a hurry, you can add several cups of ice and cold water until you fill up the jug or pitcher.

Serving Suggestions:
 The amount of sugar and the quantity of tea bags you add to your water can be modified to suit your taste. I like very strong tea, so I usually use 5-6 family sized tea bags per gallon of water, but some people only use 1. Most people seem to like my tea when I use three tea bags, which is why I recommended as many in this recipe.

 The most popular garnishes for Southern Iced Tea are lemon slices, mint leaves, or a dash of peach extract.

Run-away Broomstick
Non-Alcoholic

The Run-Away Broomstick is a wonderful fruity drink for mild weathered festivities. Because this is a non-alcoholic drink, it is great for all guests.

Ingredients
3 oz. Ginger Ale
1 tsp. Honey
2 oz. Grapefruit Juice
1 oz. Cranberry Juice
1 oz. Orange Juice

Preparation:

Blend all of the fruit juices and honey together and pour it over ice. Then, add the ginger ale and stir lightly, and enjoy!

Warm Apple Toddy

This is another great recipe for getting warm on those chilly nights. This is a great Samhain drink. While the little ones are bobbing for apples, the adults can enjoy the pleasures of apples in a different way!

Ingredients
1 ½ oz. Apple Brandy
5 oz. Apple Juice or Cider
14 Cinnamon Stick

Preparation:
Pour the brandy and apple juice (or cider) into a microwave safe mug and place the cinnamon stick in the cup with the juice and brandy. Heat until the drink is warm (usually about 30-60 seconds.)

Serving Suggestions:
To make larger quantities of this drink, pour the desired amount of brandy and apple juice into a large pot with the cinnamon sticks and warm over low heat. Serve with a ladle.

If you are serving this drink at a Samhain party where there are kids present, be sure to buy extra apple juice or cider and cinnamon sticks so the little ones can have a virgin version of this toddy.

Amaretto Hot Tea

Amaretto is wonderfully sweet and rich, which makes for a perfect after dinner dessert drink. If Amaretto is too much for your palate to handle straight, then this great recipe will allow you to enjoy Amaretto with a little more delicacy.

Ingredients
6 oz. Hot Tea
2 oz. Amaretto
Dollop of Cool-Whip® Whipped Cream

Preparation:
Pour the Tea and Amaretto into a microwave safe mug and microwave until warm (usually 30-60 seconds). Garnish with a cinnamon stick to add a zing of flavor. Note: Because Amaretto is a very rich and sweet drink, you may want to use unsweetened tea for this recipe, as it should be sweet enough.

Serving Suggestions:
If you want to serve this drink in large quantities, simply multiply the ounces of tea and amaretto by the number of guests. Or, you can make a gallon of tea and keep the bottle of Amaretto handy for guests to add their own. Some people may want more than one drink so be sure to make extra!

Chocolate Mint Hot Toddy

Chocolate and mint are two delights that blend wonderfully together and this incredibly tasty drink is a prime example of this delicious blending of flavors.

Ingredients
2 Tablespoons Cool-Whip® Whipped Cream
1 ½ oz. Peppermint Schnapps
1 Package of Hot Cocoa Mix
6 oz. Water

Preparation:

Mix the Hot Cocoa mix with hot water, and add the peppermint Schnapps. Mix with a spoon and then top the drink with a couple of tablespoons of Whipped Cream.

Serving Suggestions:

Be sure to make extra hot cocoa for the little ones if there are any children present at your event!

Black Magic Brew

This rich drink can be served either warm or cold, depending on your preference, and the weather. It's sweet and rich aroma is a pleasant delight to your senses. This recipe makes small shots of this potent, but tasty brew.

Ingredients
1 oz. Boiling Water
½ oz. Molasses
2 oz. Rum
1 Teaspoon Honey

Preparation:
Mix the boiling water, molasses, and the honey together and stir until the honey and molasses are completely dissolved, then, add the rum. Serve as it is for a warm toddy, or add crushed ice and stir once again. Strain the drink into a glass and serve.

Serving Suggestions:
You can make this drink one at a time, or for a larger batch that serves about 8 people, use the measurements below:
16 oz. Rum
4 oz. Molasses
8 tsp. Honey
8 oz. Boiling Water
Follow the above directions.

White Witch

This creamy drink is a perfect refreshment for cooling down during the summer heat.

Ingredients
1 oz. Crème de Cacao, - or Chocolate Liquor
1 oz. Vodka
½ Cup of Vanilla Ice Cream

Preparation:
Pour all of the ingredients into a blender and blend until smooth. Pour into a glass and enjoy.

Serving Suggestions:
If there are kids around, be sure to have enough ice cream on hand to make them a shake to enjoy while the adults indulge in the wonderful drink. Instead of the chocolate liquor you can use chocolate syrup, and instead of the vodka, use milk.

Crème de Menthe

This minty drink is incredible! If you enjoy mint deserts then this will most definitely hit the spot.

Ingredients
1 Pound of Fresh Mint Sprigs
4 Pints of Sugar
2 Tablespoons Peppermint Extract
1 Lemon
7 Pints of Brandy

Preparation:

Begin by chopping the mint into very small pieces. Next, peal the lemon and chop the rind into small pieces. In a bowl, (preferably a mortar and pestle) combine the mint and lemon rinds and crush them as finely as you can. Once crushed, put the crushed lemon rinds and mint into the brandy and let this soak for about a week. Next, strain the brandy several times until it runs clear. I recommend using cheesecloth to strain it. Once the brandy has been fully strained, you can now add the peppermint extract to the brandy.

In a separate pot, you will need to make a syrup, so pour in the sugar and add just enough water to melt the sugar. The amount of water you use will vary depending on the size of the pot you are using. A good guideline is to use enough water that will cover the bottom of the pot, about an inch thick. You can add more water if needed. Heat the water and sugar and stir until the sugar melts and it becomes clear and no longer cloudy. Set this aside and let it cool.

Now, add the cooled syrup to the brandy. Strain it once more if needed. It is now ready to serve or to bottle for future use.

The Apple Goddess
Non-Alcoholic

This very unique apple refreshment will leave your guests baffled at how you concocted such a delicious and different drink. It is certainly not your average apple drink!

Ingredients
4 Cups Apple Juice
½ tsp. Nutmeg
½ tsp. Coriander
½ Cups Almonds
½ tsp. Anise Seeds

Preparation:

Pour all of the ingredients into a blender and blend until smooth. You can pour it over ice and garnish with an apple slice or a crushed almond sprinkled on top.

Bananas & Berries
Non-Alcoholic

This is an incredibly tasty drink to serve in the summertime, perfect for cooling down. But not only is it tasty, it's healthy too!

Ingredients
4 oz. Orange Juice
1 Banana
¼ cup Raspberries
¼ cup Blueberries
2 oz. Milk

Preparation:

In a blender, combine all of the ingredients and blend until smooth. Then pour into a tall glass and enjoy!

Serving Suggestions:

To make this drink more fun, top the drink with fresh berries. You can also change this drink up a little by using blackberries (my favorite) instead of blueberries.

Fuzzy Lemons
Non-Alcoholic

This drink is similar to the popular drink Fuzzy Navel, yet everyone can enjoy this non-alcoholic version with a twist of lemon.

Ingredients
4 oz. Lemon Juice
6 oz. Peach Nectar
1 Cup Ice
1 Lemon (optional)

Preparation:

This is probably the simplest recipe ever. Mix the Lemon Juice with the Peach Nectar and pour over ice. You can spruce the drink up a bit by adding a slice or twist of lemon to the side of the glass.

Broom Burner Cider

This drink is great for cool or cold weather festivities held outside, as this drink is sure to keep everyone warm and toasty.

Ingredients
1 ½ oz. Whiskey
1 Cup Hot Apple Cider
1 Cinnamon Stick
1 Twist of Lemon

Preparation:
Put the cinnamon and lemon twist in a mug and pour in the whiskey, then add the hot apple cider and serve.

Kitchen Witch's Absinthe

It seems, that at almost every gathering, there are always a few people who are on a quest to make or get their hands on the perfect batch of absinthe. Being illegal because of its toxicity, absinthe has become almost like an unattainable jewel. With this recipe, you can create a less toxic, but just as potent version of absinthe that will have your guests amazed at your brewing skills.

Ingredients
2 teaspoons Wormwood
½ teaspoon Fennel seeds
2 teaspoons Anise Seeds
½ teaspoon Fennel
2 teaspoons chopped Angelica root
4 Cardamon Seeds
½ teaspoons Coriander
1 gallon of Vodka

Preparation:
All of the herbs need to be in dried form. Mix the wormwood with the vodka and let it set for about 48 hours. Then, remove the wormwood from the vodka by straining it, and once strained, add all of the other herbs to the Vodka. Let this sit for a week, and then strain again. Now, it is ready, however, many people prefer to age it a while longer, the longer, the better.

Celtic Coffee

Bailey's Irish Cream is my favorite drink for relaxing with friends, and it goes perfectly with coffee. In the summertime I prefer to enjoy a couple shots of Irish Cream straight over ice. In the wintertime, I prefer this recipe to help get warmed up.

Ingredients
4 oz. Irish Cream
4 oz. Very Strong Hot Coffee

Preparation:
Pour the coffee and the Irish Cream into a mug and enjoy!

Serving Suggestions:
You can also serve this drink cold by pouring it over ice, or refrigerating it ahead of time.

Yule Nog

Nothing raises the Yule time spirit like egg nog and this one packs a powerful Yule punch! For a great tasting non-alcoholic version, substitute the alcohol with apple juice or cider.

Ingredients
32 oz. Egg Nog
12 oz. Whiskey
1 ½ oz. Rum

Utensils / Cookware Needed:
Punch Bowl or Large Pitcher

Preparation:
This drink should be served very cold, so I recommend that you refrigerate the Egg Nog, Whiskey, and the Rum before mixing them together. Once cold, mix all of the ingredients together and let the festivities begin!

Serving Suggestions:
To make this drink look festive, you can add a tiny sprig of mint to the top of the glass.

Appetizers

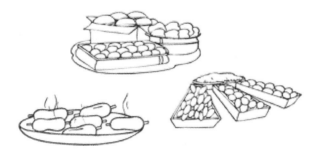

Cranberry Snowballs

A friend of mine came over several years ago with a small zip lock bag of tiny white balls. He opened the bag and took out one and told me to try one. His mother had made them that morning as one of the side dishes on a party tray. She gave him a bag full to bring to me since he was stopping by that afternoon.

I ate one of the little balls and it was just wonderful. As I crunched through it, my mouth was filled with the sweet taste of powdered sugar and the pleasantly tart taste of fresh cranberries.

Because this is one of my favorite winter time snacks, I have presented it here for you to share with your friends and family. This is also a fun treat to make with children, as it is very easy.

Ingredients
1 Bag of Cranberries
1 Cup Powdered Sugar
Utensils / Cookware Needed:
1 zip lock (or comparable bag)

Preparation:

Wash the cranberries and while they are still slightly moist, pour them into the zip lock bag. Add the sugar and shake until the cranberries are completely covered with the sugar. Next, pour the sugared cranberries onto a large plate and let them dry. The sugar will harden. You can then place them into the refrigerator and serve when ready.

Serving Suggestions:

If you have several children who would like to help you make cranberry snowballs, simply divide the cranberries up into several small bags and distribute the sugar evenly.

Something else fun that you can do is to stick the sugared cranberries onto toothpicks and stick them all over a candle. Leave the top of the candle open for the flame. When your guests arrive, light the candle and let them pick the snowballs from the candle.

Chestnut Delights

These delightful bacon covered water chestnuts are incredibly easy to prepare and taste great.

Ingredients
8 oz. Can of Water Chestnuts
1 Pound Bacon (thick cut)
Toothpicks

Preparation:
Preheat the oven to Broil. Drain the water chestnuts and set them aside. Take the bacon and cut the slices in half. Wrap the individual water chestnuts with the bacon slices and stick a toothpick through them to keep the bacon wrapped.

Put them on a baking pan and put them in the oven to broil. Turn them every few minutes as they are cooking. Cooking times will vary depending on the thickness of the bacon, so just keep checking on them and turning them until the bacon is fully cooked. This usually takes about 5 minutes.

Serving Suggestions:
Serve these tasty crispy delights with the toothpicks still in them so guests can tackle them easily.

Dill Cream Dreams

These Dill Cream Dreams, despite the name, have a delicate dill flavor which mixes great with cream cheese to make a unique and tasty appetizer. They are not too tart, and the dill really gives the cheese a savory flavor.

Ingredients
1 Package of Cream Cheese (8 oz)
1 Cylinder of Crescent Rolls (16 oz)
2 Teaspoons of Dried Dill Weed

Preparation:

Preheat the oven to 350°F (or as directed on the crescent roll package). Unroll the dough onto a lightly floured surface to prevent sticking. Lay the triangles out flat. Spread the cream cheese inside the triangles. Try and stay away from the edges and keep the cream cheese toward to the middle of the triangles to keep it from spilling out as they bake. Once the cream cheese is spread onto all of the triangles, sprinkle a small amount of dill on top of the cream cheese.

Now, roll up the crescents as directed on the package and bake according to the directions on the container, usually 15-20 minutes. Various brands may differ.

Fruit Cream Pie Dip

If you like Cheesecake, or sweetened cream cheese deserts, then you will adore this fruit dip.

Ingredients

1 Package of Soft Cream Cheese (any fruit flavored version is better - such as strawberry, pineapple, or cherry)
2 Cups Dried Cranberries
¼ Cup Apple Juice
2 Tablespoons Orange Juice
3 Cups Swiss Cheese (Shredded)

Preparation:

Preheat the oven to 375°F. Next, in a mixing bowl combine all of the ingredients and blend together until evenly mixed. Now, put the mixture into a 9" pie pan and bake for about 10-15 minutes until it is lightly browned.

Serving Suggestions:

This dip is great when served with various fruits, such as strawberries, pineapples, melons, but it is also great when spread over crackers. One of my favorite ways to enjoy this dip is to spread it over vanilla wafers.

Walnut Rounds

These little rounds taste great by themselves or on top of round crackers. They are very filling too.

Ingredients

1/3 Cup Walnuts (finely chopped)
½ Cup Butter
1 ¼ Cups Flour
4 oz. Blue Cheese
1/8 Teaspoon Salt

Preparation:

In a blender or food processor mix together the flour, blue cheese, butter and salt until it reaches as smooth consistency. Next, put the mixture in a container and mix in the walnuts. Now, split the dough in half and mold it into two long log-like shapes about two inches in diameter.

Once you have the logs molded into shape, wrap them with plastic wrap or tin foil and put them in the refrigerator for about an hour and a half, or until they begin to get firm.

Once the logs are firm, go ahead and preheat the oven to 350°F. Now, slice the logs into thin slices, about a ½ and inch thick. Arrange the slices on a cookie sheet and bake them for about 12-15 minutes.

Blue Brie

This is another recipe that is incredibly easy, yet it is absolutely delicious.

Ingredients

1 Can Blueberry Pie Filling (16 oz)
1 Wheel of Brie Cheese (Approximately 2 lbs.)

Preparation:

Preheat the oven to 350°F. Spread the brie cheese in a small baking dish or 8" pie dish. Pour the blueberry pie filling on top of the cheese and bake it for about 10-15 minutes. You really just need to cook it long enough to get good and hot.

Serving Suggestions:

This spread is great on toast, thin crackers, or vanilla wafers. It is also tasty when served with fruits.

Walnut Treasures

This recipe makes one of the tastiest little treats ever! I can sit for hours just nibbling away at these little treasures.

Ingredients
1 Pound Walnut Halves
1 Egg White
1 Teaspoon Vanilla Extract
½ Cup Brown Sugar
2 Tablespoons Cinnamon Powder
1 Teaspoon Ground Ginger
1 Teaspoon Ground Cloves

Preparation:

Begin by preheating the oven to 300°F. In a bowl, beat the egg white until it is frothy. Add all of the other ingredients EXCEPT for the walnuts. Mix this well, and then add the walnuts and stir them around until each is coated completely.

Spray a cookie sheet with non-stick spray and then spread the walnuts over the cookie sheet evenly. Bake them in the oven for about half an hour or until they are toasted.

Suggestions:

You can substitute walnuts with your favorite nuts, such as pecans or peanuts.

Tangy Bacon Swirls

If you enjoy bacon and olives, this recipe will have your taste buds rejoicing! These roll-ups are sure to please your guests and have them begging for more.

Ingredients
1 Pound Sliced Bacon
10 Slices of Bread
1 Jar Cheese Sauce (16 oz.)
1 Jar Chopped Green Olives

Preparation:

First, you will need to cut the crust off of the 10 slices of bread, and then cut the slices in half (long ways- not in triangles) and then set the slices aside. Now, you will need to cut the bacon slices in half, and set them aside.

Preheat the oven to Broil. Now, take the slices of bread and spread the cheese sauce over one side. Next, sprinkle the olives on top of the cheese. Now, roll the slices of bread up like jelly rolls. Next, wrap the rolled up slices with the ½ slices of bacon. To keep them rolled up, stick a toothpick in them.

Place the swirls on a cookie sheet and broil them in the oven for about 5 minutes, taking care to turn them often so they cook evenly and do not burn.

Ham & Pickle Roll-Ups

These are a super quick and easy appetizer to fix, especially on short notice. They require no cooking and are ready in minutes, and taste great!

Ingredients
5 Slices of Cooked Ham
5 Dill Pickle Spears
1 Package Soft Cream Cheese (8 oz.)

Preparation:

Lay the ham out flat and pat the slices dry of moisture. Next, spread the softened cream cheese on one side of the ham. Now, lay the pickle spear at the edge of the ham and roll it up like a jelly-roll. Stick three or four toothpicks (evenly spaced) through the ham and pickle to keep it rolled up, and then slice the large roll-up into smaller roll-ups by slicing between the toothpicks. You can serve these immediately or refrigerate for later.

Suggestions:

Thick ham works best for this recipe, but you could also use several thin slices of ham in the place of one thick piece per roll up.

Spicy Ham Tortilla Roll-Ups

This recipe, like the previous one, is also a quick and easy appetizer that you can fix on short notice and does not require any cooking time.

Ingredients

1 Package Soft Cream Cheese (8 oz.)
10 Ham Slices
10 Flour Tortillas
1 Jar of chunky Salsa (16 oz.)

Preparation:

Lay the slices of ham out and pat them dry to remove the moisture. Now, in a mixing bowl, combine the cream cheese with a small amount of salsa and blend until it is well mixed. Add a little more salsa, and mix again. Keep adding a little salsa at a time and mixing until it is all blended.

Spread the salsa and cheese mixture onto one side of the tortillas. Now place the ham on top. Spread a little more mixture on top of the ham slices and then roll them up like jelly-rolls. Cut them into slices and use toothpicks to hold them together.

You can serve these immediately or refrigerate them to enjoy later.

Fall Fruit Dip

This wonderful dip is perfect for dipping your favorite fruit chunks. It goes great with grapes, pineapples, cantaloupe, honey dew, watermelons, bananas and more! Its quick and easy to fix too!

Ingredients
1 Jar Marshmallow Cream (16 oz.)
1 Package Softened Cream Cheese (16 oz.)

Preparation:
The marshmallow cream and cream cheese may be a little difficult to blend if they are either cold, or room temperature. To make the blending easier, place the cheese and marshmallow cream in a microwave save dish and heat it for 15-30 seconds and then stir. Do this several times until it is completely blended.

Serving Suggestions:
Some people like to add a tablespoon of maraschino cherry juice to the dip before blending. It makes it a tad sweeter and gives it a faint pink color. This dip also goes well with vanilla wafers.

Spicy Berry Spread

This incredible spread will blow your guests away and leave a spicy, tangy, fruity taste in their mouths.

Ingredients
1 Jar Picante Sauce (16 oz.)
1 Jar Raspberry Preserves (8 oz.)
1 Package Softened Cream Cheese (8 oz.)

Preparation:

There are three ways you can prepare and serve this dish. Each is wonderful in their own right, and how you prepare it will really depend on how you want it to look, rather than taste.

1) The first method is to completely mix the picante sauce with the raspberry preserves. Then spread the cream cheese into a serving dish and simply spread the preserves/picante mixture on top of the cheese.

2) The second method is to completely mix together the picante sauce and preserves, then, swirl it together with the cream cheese; creating a marble effect. You don't blend it completely, but rather just swirl it together leaving large white areas and large dark areas.

3) The third way you can prepare this spread is to put the cream cheese, picante sauce, and the raspberry preserves into a blender or food processor, then completely blend together for a smoother, thinner spread.

Serving Suggestions:
Either of the above methods tastes great and it really depends on what kind of presentation you want to make. This spread is excellent on toast or crackers.

One idea is to prepare the swirl method above and place the mix into a bowl and surround the spread with toasted crackers.

This recipe goes well with vanilla wafers too.

Barbeque Mini Links

These are so tasty I sometimes make larger versions for dinner and put them in hotdog buns! My mother is the one who taught me this unique way of preparing little links, and even hot dog weenies.

Ingredients
2 Cups Barbeque Sauce
1 Package of Small Cocktail Weenies
2 Tablespoons Vegetable Oil

Preparation:
In a skillet, pour in the vegetable oil and begin to get the skillet hot. When it gets hot, set the heat to medium to medium high.

Place as many cocktail weenies in the pan as will fit, while leaving room to stir them around easily. Fry the weenies until the outer layer begins to get very dark, but not burnt. While they are cooking, get a plate ready to put the weenies on when they are done. Simply lay a couple of layers of paper towel onto a plate and set this aside.

When the weenies have reached a good dark color, remove them from the pan and place them on the plate with the paper towels to soak up the oil. Finish cooking the rest of the weenies.

When all of the weenies are browned, put them all back in to the pan and pour in the barbeque sauce. Stir them to get each weenie completely covered with sauce and simmer for about 5 minutes. The sauce will thicken a little.

If the initial frying pan is not large enough to put all of the weenies in, transfer the weenies and the barbeque sauce into a larger sauce pan and simmer for several minutes.

When you are done simmering the weenies in the sauce, pour them into a serving dish and spread them out so that you can stick a toothpick into each one.

Serving Suggestions:

To make larger versions of this appetizer, use your favorite hot dog weenies instead of the cocktail links.

Jalapeno Hamburger Dip

This recipe is perfect for anytime, particularly moon festivities, when you may not want to serve a formal meal, but want to give the guests a hearty appetizer that will leave them full.

Ingredients

1 Jar Sliced Jalapeno Peppers (12 oz.)
2 Pounds Ground Beef
1 Large Chopped Onion
1 Small Can Cream of Mushroom Soup
   (Small Condensed Size)
1 Pound Cheese (Cubed)

Preparation:

In a frying pan, brown the ground meat and onion together until fully cooked. Now, add the cream of mushroom soup and stir. After a few minutes when the mixture is again hot, add the cheese and stir until completely melted. Next, add the jalapenos and cook for about 10 minutes at a low simmer, taking care to stir while it is cooking.

It is now ready to serve; however, if you refrigerate this dip overnight and reheat it the next day, the juices will have blended better, making it a little spicier. If you choose to serve it the next day, then you may need to add a little milk to thin the mixture while you reheat it.

Serving Suggestions:

To make this recipe a little easier, you can substitute the cubed cheese, and instead use prepared cheese sauce, or even cheese soup.

This dip is incredible and goes well with almost any crackers, chips, or even toast, but it goes perfectly with corn chips!

Eight Blessings Dip

This incredible eight layer dip has a bit of a Mexican flair. This particular recipe is mild, but you can always spice it up a bit.

Ingredients
1 Cup of Your Favorite Salsa
1 Small Can of Black Olives (chopped – 6oz.)
1 ½ Pounds Ground Beef
1 Can Refried Beans (16 oz.)
4 Cups Shredded Monterey Jack and
     Cheddar Cheese Blend
8 oz. Sour Cream
1 Cup Guacamole
½ Cup Chopped Green Onions
½ Cup Chopped tomatoes

Preparation:

Begin by browning the Ground Beef and when it is fully cooked, set it aside for a moment. In a different bowl, mix together the olives, onions and tomatoes, and then set this aside for a moment. I've numbered the layers from bottom to top for easy reference.

1- Now, in a 9 x 13 inch sized serving tray or pan, spread the beans along the bottom.
2- Sprinkle 3 cups of the shredded cheese on top of the beans.
3- Now spread the ground beef on top of the cheese.
4- Now spread the sour cream on top of the beef.
5- Add the guacamole on top of the sour cream.
6- Now, spread the salsa over the sour cream.
7- Put the rest of the cheese on top of the sour cream.

8- Remember that bowl of olives, tomatoes & onions? Now, you can spread that mixture on top of the cheese.

Serving Suggestions:
You can adjust the spiciness of this dip by selecting either a hot or mild salsa to your liking. You can also sprinkle sliced jalapeno peppers on the top layer. Some guests may not want the added spiciness of the hot peppers though, so you can also place a small bowl of the peppers on the side, next to the dip for guests to grab as they like. This dip is great with tortilla chips.

Poseidon's Dip

Poseidon, Greek God of the Sea, must have created shrimp & crab especially for this recipe! This is another quick and easy recipe that will have your guests in line for more.

Ingredients
1 Package Soft Cream Cheese (8 oz.)
1 Jar Cocktail Sauce (8 oz.)
1 Can Small Shrimp (8 oz.)
1 Can Shredded Crab Meat (8 oz.)

Preparation:
Start by draining the shrimp and then mixing it with the cocktail sauce. Set this aside for a moment.

Now, take the cream cheese and stir it so that is very soft and creamy. Add in the crab meat to the cream cheese and stir until it is well blended.

Next lay the crab/cream cheese mixture in the center of a serving platter or dish, spreading it out. Now, pour the shrimp/cocktail sauce over the cream cheese/crab mixture.

Serving Suggestions:
This dip goes great with crackers, and especially toast.

Nordic Dip

This dip is a tasty variation from other more conventional dips, and is reminiscent of the popular Reuben sandwich.

Ingredients
8 oz. Corned Beef (Shredded)
16 oz. Sauerkraut (Drained)
16 oz. Swiss Cheese (Shredded)
½ Cup Thousand Island Dressing
½ Cup Mayonnaise

Preparation:

Begin by preheating the oven to 350° F. Now, mix together the mayonnaise and thousand island dressing.

In a 9 X 13 inch baking pan, spread out the sauerkraut. Now, layer the corned beef on top of the sauerkraut. Then, layer the Swiss cheese on top of the beef. Next, layer the dressing-mayonnaise mixture on top of the sauerkraut. Now you are ready to put the pan in the oven and bake for 20-25 minutes.

Serving Suggestions:

Nordic Dip goes perfectly with small slices of toasted rye bread, or wheat crackers.

Green God Nibblers

These little nibblers are very tasty and very popular with guests. They are filling and your guests will be satisfied and delighted. You may want to make sure that you make enough of these little nibblers, because you will find that you will run out quickly!

Ingredients

5 Cups Vegetable Oil
3 ½ Cups Dry Bread Crumbs
4 Cups Shredded Cheddar Cheese (Sharp)
1 Package Chopped Frozen Broccoli – 16 oz.
   (thawed out and drained)

Preparation:

Heat up the oil in a deep frying pan or in a deep fryer. If you can control the temperature, try for 375° F.

While you are getting the oil ready, place the broccoli in a separate saucepan with 1 ½ Cups water. Cook the broccoli for about 5 minutes. Make sure the broccoli is not cooked too long or it will become too limp. You want it to be firm.

Now, in another saucepan, melt the cheddar cheese over low heat until it is completely melted and then add in the cooked broccoli and stir until the broccoli is completely covered. Set this aside and let it cool for about 20 minutes.

Once the broccoli and cheese have thickened, dip the broccoli bits individually into the bread crumbs and coat them by rolling them around.

You are now ready to deep fry the balls. Fry them for about 5 minutes or until golden brown. Drain the oil from the bits by placing them onto paper towels. Add salt and pepper to taste.

Serving Suggestions:

These little nibblers are great by themselves, but I enjoy dipping them in ranch dressing, so you may want to set out a small dish of ranch beside your platter.

Hekate's Gift

The ingredients in this recipe, when combined, have a strong Greek flair, so I named this tantalizing appetizer after one of our favorite & powerful Greeks, Hekate.

Ingredients
1 Cup Black Olives
12 oz. Goat Cheese
1 Cup Diced Sun-Dried Tomatoes
3 Cloves Garlic
4 Tablespoons Fresh Basil (Chopped)
2 Tablespoons Fresh Rosemary (Chopped)
¼ Cup Olive Oil

Preparation:

Cut the goat cheese into squares that are about one inch. Spread them out into a pan and set them aside for a moment.

Take the garlic cloves and chop them into evenly sized pieces. You will be pushing the pieces inside the cheese, so you will not want to get the pieces too large. If you know how large a clove is, you can use a clove as a guideline for how large the garlic pieces should be. Once you have the cloves cut into pieces, now push them into the cheese squares with a toothpick. One piece of clove per square if you want a mild garlic flavor, or two pieces if you want a stronger garlic flavor.

Once you have all of the squares filled with garlic, spread the olives, sun-dried tomatoes, basil and rosemary on top of the cheese squares.

Cover the pan and let it set in the refrigerator overnight to blend the juices and marinate.

Tip:
When picking out your olive oil, I would recommend that you not get extra-virgin olive. It tends to be too strong. I would recommend a mild or light oil.

Serving Suggestions:
These wonderful cheese squares go great with crackers. You could also make larger slices for putting on sliced garlic bread or toast. Use the same ingredients as above, except instead of the small one inch cheese squares, use large thick slices.

You could also lay the larger slices onto the garlic bread slices and warm in the oven for several minutes until the cheese begins to melt for a more formal and hearty dish.

Asgard Spread

Asgard can be interpreted by some as the Astru, or Nordic equivalent of Heaven. And since I've heard many people call this spread heavenly, I decided to give it a more fitting title!

Ingredients
16 oz. Cream Cheese, Softened
4 Cups Shredded Monterey Jack Cheese
4 oz. Deviled Ham (2 Small cans)
1 Teaspoon Soy Sauce
4 Tablespoons Milk
4 Tablespoons Chopped Green Onions

Preparation:
Mix all of the above ingredients together and place it in a serving tray.

Serving Suggestions:
This spread is best served when chilled, so refrigerate it for a couple of hours if possible before serving.
This is another dip/spread that goes very well with tortilla chips, but this one will also go good with toast, or crackers.

Main Courses

Hamburger Stew

This recipe is one I learned by watching my mother. She would cook this stew when the whole family was due to arrive and there were a lot of mouths to feed. I now fix this wonderful stew for my own family and friends. It is very easy to fix and tastes great, so I'm sure you will enjoy it too.

Ingredients
1 Large can Veg-All (Vegetable assortment)
1 Small can potatoes
1 Small can peas (your favorite peas)
1 Medium can stewed tomatoes
1 small can of corn
2 Tablespoons Chili Powder
1 Teaspoon salt
Water
1 Pound Ground Beef

Preparation:

Cook the meat in the pot until it has browned. Pour off most of the grease, leaving a little for flavor. Add all of the vegetables, potatoes, peas, corn, and tomatoes. Now fill the pot up with water until it gets about two or three inches from the top of the pot – you need to leave room for the stew to boil without boiling over. Add the salt and chili powder and stir well. Bring the stew to a rolling boil for about five minutes. Now let the stew simmer for about twenty minutes. You can add more chili powder and salt to suite your taste.

Serving Suggestions:

I have intentionally left the precise measurements out of this recipe. Every pot of stew is different and you can substitute some of the vegetable for ones you like better, like green beans, or you can add more of the vegetables that are listed.

This stew goes well with corn bread and a slice of onion on the side. It is very hearty, so I rarely use side dishes when serving it, as it alone is very filling.

Shepherd's Pie

I came up with this recipe after eating something similar at my friend Shannon's house one evening. She prepared hers a little differently, using beef chunks instead of ground beef, adding carrots to the potatoes, and she doesn't use a crust. Both versions are great, but each a little different. My family prefers my recipe because it's a little cheesier and is an actual savory pie with crust and all.

Ingredients
1 Pound ground beef
4 Servings Instant Mashed Potatoes
   (Will also need milk, butter and salt according to the directions on the potatoes)
8-12 oz. Shredded / Grated Cheese
½ tsp. Salt
½ tsp. Onion Powder (for the meat)
½ tsp. Onion Powder (for the potatoes)
½ tsp. Cinnamon Powder
2 Frozen (flour) Pie Crusts – Ready to cook
1 tsp. Paprika (optional)

Preparation:
Preheat the oven and cook the pie crusts according the directions on the package (usually at 350 for 12 minutes). Be sure to poke tiny holes in the crust with a fork before baking, else you will have large bubbles to form while it bakes. While the pie crusts are baking, brown the meat in a skillet. As the meat begins to get good and brown, add the salt, onion powder and cinnamon and continue to cook the meat until is fully cooked. Be sure not to let the meat get overcooked, or too dry.

Once the meat is done, the pie crusts should be able ready to pull out of the oven, so set the crusts aside for now, but leave the oven on because you will need it again in a moment.

Now, you will need to prepare the mashed potatoes. Use the directions on the package to prepare the potatoes, making at least four servings. When you have finished making the mashed potatoes, set it aside for the moment.

Lay out the two pie crust and begin filling them in like so:

**Layer a thin layer of shredded cheese on the bottom of the crust.

**Split the meat in half and put ½ in one crust and the other ½ in the other pie crust on top of the cheese.

**On top of the meat, place another layer of cheese, thicker this time (much thicker!)

**On top of the thicker cheese, spread ½ of the mashed potatoes onto one pie, and the rest on the other pie.

**Top the mashed potatoes with a thin layer of cheese and then sprinkle the finished pies with paprika to add a hint of color and mild flavoring.

Serving Suggestions:

Cinnamon? You think I'm crazy right? Well, don't knock it until you've tried it! I got the idea of adding a bit of cinnamon to this recipe after eating a similar dish at a Greek restraint. The owner said the secret was to add a dash of cinnamon to the ground meat to give it a woodsy flavor. It makes all the difference, and I guarantee that by using this recipe, your Shepherd's Pie will taste better than anyone's!

You might not want to mention to people that you added cinnamon to it, at least not before they eat it. They will be expecting it to taste like a cinnamon roll! Which, I promise, it will not.

Avocado Wraps

These wraps are great! They are very hearty and easy to make. This recipe serves five but you can adjust the recipe easily to accommodate fewer or more people.

Ingredients
10 Slices of Cooked Bacon
5 Flour Tortillas
1 Avocado (Pealed, pitted & sliced or diced)
5 Tablespoons Ranch Dressing
1 Tomato (Diced)
1 Cup Shredded Lettuce
Salt & Pepper to Taste

Preparation:
Crumble the bacon into small chunks and set this aside. Lay out the tortillas and spread ranch dressing on one side of the tortillas. Now, in a line down the center of the tortilla lay the lettuce, tomato, bacon and avocado. Add salt and pepper to taste and then roll the tortilla up and serve.

Serving Suggestions:
You can add hot peppers to these wraps for a spicier flavor. You can buy precooked bacon at the store to cut your preparation time down.

Meatballs Deluxe With Spaghetti

This is a very filling meal and one of my family's favorites. I hope you enjoy it as much as we do!

Ingredients

For the Meatballs:
2 ½ Pounds Ground Beef
1 Cup Instant Rice
1 Teaspoon Garlic Salt
2 Eggs
1 Can of Condensed Tomato Soup (26 oz.)
26 oz. Water
1 Cup Mozzarella Cheese (Shredded)
1 Teaspoon Dried Basil

For the Spaghetti:
1 Package of your Favorite Spaghetti
1 Jar of your favorite Spaghetti Sauce

Preparation:

Prepare the spaghetti according to the directions on the package. When the spaghetti is fully cooked, drain it and then pour 3 Tablespoons of the Olive Oil onto the spaghetti and mix this well. The oil will prevent the spaghetti from becoming sticky until it is served.

Warm the spaghetti sauce in a separate pot and set it aside for the time being.

Begin preparing the meatballs by beating the eggs. Now, mix together the rice, beef, Basil, Garlic Salt, and the eggs, until they are completely blended. You will have to use your hands for this.

When the mixture is blended, shape the mix into medium sized meatballs, about an inch and half big in diameter.

In a saucepan, pour in the tomato soup and begin to warm it. When it gets warm, add a can of water and bring it to a simmering boil.

Drop in the meatballs into the soup and cook over a low simmer for about 30 minutes.

Remove the meatballs when they are cooked, and put them onto your serving tray. Drizzle some of the soup on top. Now, scatter the mozzarella cheese on top of the meatballs and stick toothpicks through them.

Serving Suggestions:
When I serve this dish, I usually offer garlic bread on the side. I also leave the spaghetti sauce, spaghetti, and the meatballs in separate pots so the guests may dish out the amount of each that they want.

Some people may not want meatballs, and some will want a lot, so it's best to let them decide how much of what they would like.

Chicken Casserole

This recipe was passed onto me by my Mother, who sometimes uses tuna instead of chicken. Both recipes are great. This is one of my favorite dishes.

Ingredients
1 Medium Can Diced Tomatoes
4 Small Cans of Chicken
1 ½ Cups Instant Rice
1 Family Sized Can of Cream of Chicken
1 Cup of Shredded Cheddar Cheese
1 Cup of Crushed Potato Chips
1/3 Cup Green Olives
½ Cup Water
½ Whole Onion

Preparation:

Preheat the oven to 350° F.

In a large baking pan, grease the sides and then pour in the rice. Drain the juice from the tomatoes onto the rice and then add half of the diced tomatoes. Add the water and stir this up well. Slice the onion into rings and lay the rings on top of the rice mixture.

Sprinkle the chicken on top of the rice & onions and then pour the cream of chicken soup on top of the chicken.

Sprinkle on the cheese evenly, and then sprinkle on the crushed potato chips. Now sprinkle the rest of the tomatoes and then the olives on top of the chips.

Bake this in the oven for about 30 minutes and serve warm.

Serving Suggestions:

If you want to make tuna casserole instead of chicken, it's very simple to make the switch. Instead of the cans of chicken, replace these with cans of tuna.

Instead of the cream of chicken soup, for the tuna casserole you should use cream of mushroom soup. Everything else remains the same, and both are very tasty.

Sweet Summer Solstice Chops

Another Southern favorite of mine is Pork Chops. This recipe is my favorite way to prepare pork chops, as it gives your taste buds a delicious, delightful, sweet ride, and it is something you can cook and pack up and carry to an event and it still tastes delicious hours later.

Ingredients
5-6 Pork Chops (Medium thickness)
½ Cup (or more) Brown Sugar
5-6 Tablespoons Butter
5-6 Tablespoons Soy Sauce
1 Cup Water

Utensils / Cookware Needed:
Large Baking Pan
Aluminum Foil
Preparation:
Preheat the oven to 400°. Pour the water into the pan and lay the pork chops flat into the water. On each pork chop sprinkle a tablespoon of soy sauce. Then, on each pork chop lay a tablespoon of butter. Then sprinkle the brown sugar on top of the chops. Cover the pan with the foil and bake for 15-20 minutes.
Serving Suggestions:
Pork Chops go great with turnip greens, black eyed peas, corn bread, and iced tea. This recipe can be divided up, or increased very easily. The key is that you have at least one tablespoon each of brown sugar, butter, and soy sauce for each pork chop cook, and just put enough water in the pan to cover the bottom to help keep the chops moist while cooking.

Jambalaya

This is a wonderful tasting and very filling dish. When I serve it, I usually don't prepare side dishes, as it perfect by itself.

Ingredients
½ Pound Sausage
   (Sliced with casings removed)
½ Pound Chicken
   (Cut into large chunks 1-2 inches long.)
½ Pound cooked Shrimp
2 Tablespoons Vegetable Oil
1 Can Condensed French Onion Soup (10.5 oz)
½ Can of Water
   (From the French Onion Soup Can)
1/3 Picante Sauce
½ Cup Frozen Peas
1 Cup Instant White Rice
2 Garlic Cloves (chopped)
½ Cup Diced Tomatoes

Preparation:

In a large skillet, begin to heat the oil and then add in the garlic, chicken and the sausage and cook until browned.

Once the meat has browned, add in the onion soup, the ½ can of water, and the picante sauce and bring this to a boil. Let this boil for a couple of minutes, then add in the rice, shrimp, tomatoes, and the peas.

Now, cover the skillet and boil at a low simmer for about 5 minutes.

Serving Suggestions:

Add salt and pepper to taste and it is ready to serve. Many people who enjoy this dish prefer it to be a bit spicier. To remedy this, you can have a small jar of Red Pepper on hand for guests to adjust the taste to their liking.

If you want to offer your guests side dishes with this Jambalaya, you can go the traditional route and offer corn on the cob, corn bread, turnip greens, or any number of home-style southern treats.

Garlic Butter Spaghetti

This recipe is one that I created while trying to recreate a dish I enjoyed while eating at a restaurant called the Pot Pie Pizzeria located in Houston. It is a very simple and inexpensive dish to create, regardless if you have two or twenty-five people to feed.

Ingredients
1 package Spaghetti
3 Heaping Tablespoons Butter
1 Teaspoon Garlic Salt (you may adjust this to your preference.)

Utensils / Cookware Needed:
Large Pot

Preparation:
Prepare the spaghetti according to the directions on the package. Drain the prepared spaghetti and while the spaghetti is still hot, add the butter, stirring until it is completely melted. Now add the garlic salt to suit your taste.

Serving Suggestions:
You can serve this as a completely vegetarian dish with garlic bread or rolls, or you can serve meatballs on the side.

Desserts

Caramel Apple Pecan Pie

This is a most delicious recipe that you are sure to enjoy. I make these pies almost every year and give them out to friends and relatives. I found something similar at my local grocery store several years back and came up with this very similar recipe.

Ingredients
1 Pre-made Flour Pie Crust (ready to bake)
1 Can Apple Pie Filling
1 Cup Halved or Quartered Pecans
1 Teaspoon Cinnamon
½ Cup Caramel Sauce
¼ Cup Brown Sugar

Preparation:
Fill the pie crust with the apple pie filling and sprinkle the cinnamon on top. Sprinkle the pecans on top of the apples and then sprinkle with brown sugar.

Bake the pie in the oven according to the directions on the apple pie filling canister.

When the pie is finished cooking, let it cool. Drizzle the caramel sauce onto the individual pie slices before serving.

Note:
If you add the caramel sauce to the pie and then refrigerate, the sauce may begin to turn white and get runny. This is why I recommend that you add the caramel to the individual slices before serving.

Serving Suggestions:
The caramel that you use for this recipe can be any kind you would like. I prefer to use the same kind of caramel that one would put on top of ice cream. You can even make your own by melting caramel squares, but this will add to your preparation time.

Peach Delight

This recipe is a variation of cobbler, but everyone who has ever tried it has told me that it is better than any cobbler they have ever eaten! I hope you enjoy it.

Ingredients
1 Package Yellow Cake Mix
1 Large Can of Peaches
1 Stick of Butter
1 Cup of Sugar

Preparation:
Preheat the oven to 350° F. Pour the Large Can of Peaces into a 9 X 13 baking dish. Sprinkle the cake mix on top of the peaches, but do not mix.

Slice the stick of butter into pats (about a tablespoon each) and place them on top of the powdered cake mix – evenly spaced.

Now sprinkle the sugar on top of the butter and cake mixture. Again, do not mix.

Bake in the oven for about 20-30 minutes, or until golden brown.

Serving Suggestions:
This dish is great either hot or cold, and goes great with ice cream.

Pink Cream Salad

This is another very easy recipe with almost no prep time involved. No cooking, and it taste absolutely wonderful and refreshing.

Ingredients

2 Large Tubs of Coo-Whip® Whipped Cream
1 Small Box of Cherry Kool-Aid® Powder Mix
1 Medium sized can of mixed fruit - drained
    (Fruit Salad- you can use a larger can for more fruit to suit your preference.)
½ Cup Walnuts or Pecans (Chopped)
½ Cup Pitted Cherries (Drained if jarred)

Preparation:

Combine the 2 tubs of whipped cream with the package of cherry Kool-Aid mix and blend this until it is evenly mixed together. Now mix in the fruit, cherries, and the nuts.

Cover and refrigerate for at least two hours before serving so that the fruit has time to chill.

Serving Suggestions:

You can add any fruit you would like to this recipe as there is no exact science to it. It's all up to you and what you prefer.

Best Ever Lemon Pie

This recipe is the one my mother uses to prepare our family's favorite lemon pies. This incredibly creamy and rich pie is sure to be a hit at your next gathering of friends and family!

Ingredients

1 Lemon
3 Tablespoons Sugar
1 Tub Whipped Cream (Cool-Whip®)
1 Pre-made Frozen Pie Crust (Flour – 9 inch)
1 Can Sweetened Condensed Milk (14 oz.)
½ Cup Lemon Juice
2 Egg Yolks

Preparation:

Prepare the pie crust and bake it according to the directions on the pie crust package. Allow it to cool a bit before pouring in the filling.

While the pie crust is cooling, you can begin to prepare the filling. In a separate bowl, beat the egg yolks. Once beaten, add the condensed milk and stir until smooth. Now, add in the lemon juice and stir until completely blended. It will begin to thicken as you stir it, and when it becomes very thick (but not too thick to prevent pouring) pour it into the pie shell and spread it out evenly. Refrigerate for an hour or two before serving.

When you are ready to serve the pie, prepare the following for the topping.

For the whipped cream, you can either spread it evenly over the entire pie, or you can plop a couple of large tablespoons worth onto each slice as you serve it.

Now, cut the lemon into thick 1/2 slices and then cut the slices in half. (Make sure you have the same amount of lemon slices as you will have of the pieces of pie.) Once you have the slices cut in half, dip the slices in the sugar making sure you have the lemon covered on both sides. Stick one lemon slice in the top of each pie piece and serve.

Serving Suggestions:
　　　　This pie is very rich so you may want to make the slices small. In Texas, we like things big and I usually cut my pies to have pretty large slices, but with this pie, it's best to start small, and then let the guests have another if they can handle it. This is absolutely the best lemon pie I have ever tasted and I hope you enjoy it too!

Chocolate Pudding Pie

　　　　This is one of the easiest pie recipes, and it's quick to prepare. It makes a perfect summertime treat on those hot afternoons, when you don't want to spend a lot of time in the kitchen.

Ingredients
2 Packages of Chocolate Instant Pudding
　　　　Powder Mix
Milk (Approximately 3 ½ Cups – See Below)
Whipped Cream (Cool Whip®)
1 Pre-made Deep Dish Pie Crust (Frozen)

Optional Additions:
Chocolate Sprinkles

Preparation:

Bake the pie crust according to the instructions on the package. When the pie crust has cooled, you can now begin to prepare the filling.

The amount of milk you need will depend on the pudding directions. Most instant pudding mixes call for 2 cups of milk per package. Because we are going to make this into a pie, the pudding will need to be a little bit firmer, so I recommend using ¼ cup less milk per package than what is recommended on the pudding instructions. If your pudding box says to use 2 cups per package, then I would recommend that you use 3 ½ cups of milk for this recipe since you will be using two boxes of pudding.

Now, prepare the pudding as indicated above, and pour it into the cooled pie shell, and smooth it out over the crust. Refrigerate the pie for about an hour until it begins to become firm. Now you are ready to add the whipped cream.

Serving Suggestions:

You can either add the whipped cream to the entire pie then top it with chocolate sprinkles, or you can leave the whipped cream off, and add the whipped cream to individual slices as you serve them, adding the sprinkles piece by piece.

Home Style Banana Pudding

This is one of my favorite desserts! The creamy coolness is perfect for hot days during the summer and it is pretty simple to prepare.

Ingredients
2 Boxes of Powdered Banana Pudding Mix
4 Cups Milk
½ Box of Vanilla Wafers
3 Bananas
1 Tub of Cool Whip® Whipped Cream

Preparation:
Begin by spreading ¼ box of Vanilla Wafers on the bottom of the pan or large bowl that you will be serving the pudding in.

Now, peel and slice the bananas into half inch slices and spread the slices along the top of the wafers.

In a different bowl, mix the milk and pudding mix until it is well blended. Let this set for about three minutes until it becomes a little bit thicker.

Spoon the banana pudding over the wafers and bananas.

Stick the rest of the vanilla wafers (1/4 of the box) along the edge of the pudding to create a wafer edging around the bowl or dish.

It is now ready to refrigerate. Serve cold.

Serving Suggestions:
If the pudding mix is too thin when you pour it over the bananas, the bananas may rise to the top, as well as the wafers. This is fine, but you will need to poke them back to the bottom so that they are submerged within the pudding, else they will begin to blacken quickly if left on the top exposed to the air.

Spread the whipped cream on top of the pudding and add more wafers for decoration.

Chocolate Pudding Cake

This recipe is one I learned from my grandmother. There is not a dessert on earth I enjoy more than a piece of this cake with a tall glass of milk.

Ingredients
1 Box of Chocolate Cake
1 Box of Powdered Instant Chocolate
 Pudding Mix
1 Cup of Chocolate Chips
(You will also need the ingredients listed on the back of the cake mix)

Optional Additions:
2 Cans of Milk Chocolate Icing

Utensils / Cookware Needed:
Bunt Pan (or 2 - 9" round baking pans)

Preparation:
Preheat the oven according to the directions on the cake mix package. Prepare the cake mix according to the directions on the package. Once the mix is prepared, add the package of dry pudding mix and mix until there are no lumps. Now, add the chocolate chips and stir.

From this point on, you can choose which kind of cake you would like to make. You can make a coffee type cake by baking it in a bunt pan and leaving off the icing.

Or you can make a traditional two- layer cake by baking the cake in two 9" round pans. If you choose this method, bake the cakes according to the directions on the box, then let the two cakes cool when they are done. Once cool, use one can of icing to spread on the top and sides of the first cake. Once it is completely covered, place the second cake on top of the first cake, and continue to cover it in icing as you did the first cake, until it is completely covered.

Serving Suggestions:
    To make this cake more ornamental, you can add a few chips to the top if you chose to cover it in icing. This cake is very rich and delicious, regardless if you bake a bunt or two layer version of it.

Luscious Lemon Delights

This lemony cold treat is great for summer events when you need to cool down. It's easy to prepare and will have your guests begging for seconds.

Ingredients
1 Package Neufchatel Cheese, Softened (8oz.)
1 Package Lemon Flavored Gelatin Mix (3 oz)
1 ½ Cups Boiling Water
1 Teaspoon Lemon Zest (Grated)
2 Cups Cool-Whip® Whipped Cream
1/3 Cup Frozen Lemonade Concentrated

Preparations:
    Begin by thawing the lemonade. Once thawed, set it aside for now. In a bowl, combine the lemon gelatin mix with the boiling water and stir. Set this aside for a moment.
    In a separate bowl, beat together the lemonade concentrate, the Neufchatel cheese, and the lemon zest until it is smooth. Now stir in the gelatin mix and chill while you finish preparing the molds. For the molds, you can use a 6 cup muffin pan. Grease each cup with butter and then set this aside. Now, fold together the whipped cream and the lemon gelatin/cheese mixture. Next, spoon the mixture into the molds and chill overnight. Turn over onto a serving tray and serve cold.

Amazing Banana Sorbet

This recipe is very simple, yet it makes for an amazing summer dessert. There are only three ingredients, but you will receive ten times as many compliments over this cool treat when served to your guests!

Ingredients
3 Bananas
1 Cup Very Hot Water
1 Cup Sugar

Preparation:

Begin my mixing together the hot water with the sugar and stir it until the mixture turns clear and the sugar has completely melted. Remove from the heat and let this mixture begin to cool while you prepare the bananas.

Now in a separate bowl, peel the three bananas and begin to mash them up until you have a bowl of banana mush.

When the syrup has cooled down a bit, stir in the bananas and mix together well.

Pour the mixture into a freezer safe container and put it in the freezer for several hours. Take it out and stir it up, then put back in the freezer for several more hours. Once it is set, it is ready to serve.

Winter Moon Compote

The ingredients in this recipe blend together so perfectly to create a delicious topping to any fruit dessert such as cobbler, ice cream, or even chicken and pork chops. I especially enjoy smothering this compote on top of a slice of coffee cake.

I was told that the original version of this recipe was from the McCormick Company but that mine was just a little bit different. I received this recipe from a friend and have not used the McCormick recipe, but I'm sure they are both equally delicious. I know this was is!

Ingredients
1 Cup Raisins
1 Cup Dried Cranberries
1 Cup Dried Figs (Sliced in fourths)
1 Cup Dried Apricots (Sliced in fourths)
½ Cups Brown Sugar (light)
2 Cups Apple Juice
2 Tablespoons Lemon Juice
½ Cup Water
2 Teaspoons Vanilla Extract
1 Teaspoon Ground Cinnamon
1 Teaspoon Ground Ginger

Preparation:

Pour the water, apple juice, lemon juice and the brown sugar into a saucepan and simmer over medium heat until the brown sugar has completely dissolved. Be sure to stir the mixture frequently while it simmers so as not to let the sugar burn at the bottom of the pot. Once the sugar has completely melted, add all of the dried fruits, vanilla extract, and the spices.

Once you have added all of the ingredients, simmer it over a low boil for about 5-7 minutes until the fruits begin to plum up a little bit, and the juice begins to become a little bit thicker.

Remove from the heat and let the mixture cool. Then refrigerate the mixture in a covered container until you are ready to serve.
Serving Suggestions:
This compote is wonderful over pound cake, coffee cake, ice creams, cobblers, and pies.

Nutty Chocolate Drops

These little candies are very easy to prepare and the will disappear quickly so be sure to make plenty!
Ingredients
3 Cups Crisp Rice Cereal
2 Pounds Chocolate Almond Bark® Squares
2 Cups Roasted Peanuts
1 Cup Peanut Butter
2 Cups Marshmallows (miniature)
Preparation:
Begin by melting the Almond Bark in the microwave. Heat it for a short time (30 seconds) and stir, keep doing this until it is completely melted.

Now, stir the peanut butter in and mix it together until completely blended. Next, add the marshmallows, peanuts, rice, and stir this together until it is blended evenly.

On a cookie sheet covered with wax paper, drop large dollops of the mix to make little dumpy cookies. Refrigerate them until you are ready to serve.
Serving Suggestions:
You can substitute the peanuts for other nuts, or even add other nuts in addition to the peanuts. If you add too many things though, you may need to compensate by adding a little more almond bark to hold everything together.For variety, you could add chocolate chips, peanut butter chips, raisins, or any other treat you like. This recipe is very easy to modify because you just throw in what you like!

Chewy Choco Logs

This recipe is reminiscent of the popular Tootsie Rolls®, but it's a little bit different. Many people have said that these are better, so I'll let you be the judge.

Ingredients
½ Cup Light Corn Syrup
2 Tablespoons Butter (Melted)
2 Squares Unsweetened Bakers Chocolate
1 Teaspoon Vanilla Extract
¾ Cup Powdered Milk
3 Cups Powdered Sugar

Preparation:
   Begin by melting the butter and the chocolate. Once melted, combine the butter and chocolate and mix until well blended. Then add the corn syrup, vanilla, powdered milk, and 2 cups of the powdered sugar and blend together.
   By this time the dough will start to become very stiff. Let it sit for a few minutes so that it will become a little bit softer. On your work area, sprinkle the rest of the powdered sugar on the surface and knead the dough until the rest of the sugar has been worked into the dough. Again, the dough will become very stiff, so letting it sit for a minute will make it a bit easier to work with. Now, pinch off small balls of the dough and shape them into little logs. (Read over the Serving Suggestions below to decide what size logs you will need.) When you have finished shaping all of the dough, you can wrap them in wax paper to help them retain their shape.

Serving Suggestions:
   After these have cooled, you can go a step further by decorating them. If you are feeling artistic, you could get some red and green cake icing and turn

these little logs into festive little Choco Yule Logs by adding tiny green holy leaves and red berries and/or a red ribbon. If you decide that you may want to decorate them, it may be better to make the logs a bit larger so they are easier to work with, otherwise, you may have to make microscopic sized decorations that no one would be able to see!

If you decide to make the little Yule Logs, there is no need to wrap them in wax paper individually, since this would ruin the decorations, but you may want to put them onto a serving dish and cover the whole dish with wax paper until you are ready to serve.

No Bake Blueberry Squares

This is a great cheesecake-like dessert that requires no baking. It makes a beautiful presentation too and is perfect for impressing your guests with your talents in the kitchen!

Ingredients:
For the Crust:
3 Tablespoon Sugar
1 ½ Cups Graham Cracker Crumbs
½ Cup of Melted Butter

For the Filling:
1 Package Soft Cream Cheese (8 oz.)
3 Cups Frozen Blueberries
1 Tub Whipped Cream (8 oz.)
1 Cup Sugar
½ Teaspoon Lemon Juice
¼ Teaspoon Salt
2 Teaspoons Vanilla Extract

Preparation:

Grease a 9 X 13 baking pan with butter. To prepare the crust, mix together the sugar, graham cracker crumbs, and the butter until they are completely blended. Sprinkle the mixture in the bottom of the pan and then press together creating a firm crust. Then, set this aside for now.

In a different bowl, mix together the cream cheese with the sugar until it is smooth, then mix in the lemon juice and salt. Fold in the whipped cream, then the blueberries.

Now, spread the mixture evenly over the crust into the pan. Cover the pan and then refrigerate overnight if possible. If you need the dessert sooner, try and refrigerate at least and hour or two before serving.

Divine Cheesecake Lemon Bars

I am a lover of cheesecake and these little bars are absolutely divine. If you enjoy cream cheese desserts, and if you like lemon, you will go crazy for these! I cam across this recipe from a friend and have kept it handy ever since.

Ingredients:

For the Crust:

1/3 Cup Sugar
1 ½ Cups Graham Cracker Crumbs
1/3 Cup Pecans (Finely Chopped)
1/3 Cup Melted Butter

For the Filling:

1 Can Sweetened Condensed Milk (14 oz)
2 Packages Soft Cream Cheese (8 oz. each)
½ Cup Concentrated Lemon Juice
2 Eggs

Preparation:

Begin by preheating the oven to 350°F.

Now, in a bowl, combine the melted butter with the graham cracker crumbs, pecans, and sugar. Blend this until it is mixed well. Set this aside for a moment. Next, in a 9 X 13 inch pan, sprinkle the crumb mixture onto the bottom and then press together until firm, creating a crust.

Now, in a separate bowl, beat together the cream cheese and the condensed milk until they are smoothly blended. Now, add in the eggs, and continue to mix. Once blended, add in the lemon juice and continue to blend together.

Now, spread the mixture over the crust until it is evenly distributed. Be careful not to disturb the crust and spread it slowly out.

Put the pan in the oven and bake for about 30 minutes. Once cooked, let the pan cool and then refrigerate for about 2 hours until it is very firm. Once firm, slice it into bars and serve.

Coffee Can Ice Cream

No, this is not Coffee flavored Ice Cream, but rather, this is a delicious Vanilla Ice Cream that is made by using coffee cans. This is a perfect project to entertain children with, and the results of the fun are tasty to everyone!

Ingredients
2 Quarts Half-and-Half Cream
½ Pint Heavy Cream
1 ½ Cups White Sugar
4 Teaspoons Vanilla Extract
1 Pinch Salt

Several Packages of Ice Cream Rock Salt
Bag of Crushed Ice
Several Large Empty Coffee Cans with Lids
Same Number of Small Empty Coffee
    Cans with Lids

Preparation:

Mix together the creams, sugar, extract, and the pinch of salt until they are well blended.

Now with the small coffee cans (clean of course) pour in the ice cream mixture, leaving about two inches empty from the top. Close the lids and set the cans inside the larger Coffee cans. Pour the rock salt between the large can and the small can, about a half inch thick, and then add several inches of ice. Add more rock salt, then more ice and keep layering them until the cans are full.

Now put the lids onto the large coffee cans and call the kids!

Have the kids roll the cans along the floor or ground. I usually help the kids out, but I don't care for getting on the ground and rolling them around, so instead, I find a chair, and place the cans under my feet and roll them back and forth with my feet. (Yeah, I know, that's the lazy way of doing it, but it gives my legs a good work out!)

After about ten minutes, open the cans up and check the ice cream. You may want to give them a quick stir. Then, add more ice and salt, close the lids and keep rolling them.

If the kids get tired of rolling them, you can always cheat and stick the cans in the freezer for a bit, making sure to stir them every hour or so until they are frozen.

If you stick to the coffee can method, you will end up with a soft and creamy ice cream, but if you go with the freezer method, it will be a lot stiffer. Either way is delicious!

You can also use a mechanical ice-cream maker of course!

Peanut Butter Ice Cream

Peanut Butter Ice Cream is my favorite! I hope you enjoy it as I do. This is a tasty and unique treat.

Ingredients
3 Cups Milk
4 Cups Half-and-Half Cream
3 Cups Powdered Milk
4 Teaspoons Vanilla Extract
1 ½ Cups Sugar
1 ½ Cups Peanut Butter

Preparation:

In a saucepan, mix together the half and half, powdered milk and the vanilla extract and heat this over low heat until the powdered milk has dissolved. Now, stir in the sugar and the peanut butter and heat over low until the sugar has melted and peanut butter is completely blended. Now, remove the mixture from the heat and place it in the refrigerator to cool.

Once the mixture has cooled, stir it again and proceed to making the ice cream in your preferred manner. You can either use a mechanical ice cream maker, or you can use the coffee can method mentioned in the previous recipe, or you can place it in the freezer, taking care to stir it every hour or so until it is frozen solid.

Scrumptious S'mores

Almost everyone loves S'mores and this recipe is sure to please everyone! This recipe is easy to prepare and taste great.

Ingredients
2 Cups Semisweet Chocolate Chips
3 Cups Marshmallows (Miniature)
3 Cups Graham Cracker Crumbs
1/3 Cup Sugar
1 Cup Butter (Melted)

Preparation:

Begin by preheating the oven to 350°F. Now, in a bowl, stir together the melted butter, sugar, and the crumbs until they are completely blended. Divide the mixture in half. Press half of the mixture in a greased 9 X 9 pan and press together until the crust is firm.

Now, pour the chocolate chips evenly over the crust. Next, sprinkle the marshmallows over the chocolate chips. Now, sprinkle the rest of the crumb mixture over the top of the marshmallows and press it together firmly with either your hand or a spatula.

Put the pan in the oven and bake it for about 10 minutes or until the chocolate and marshmallows begin to melt. Let it cool completely before you cut into squares.

Peanut Butter Cookies

Because I love peanut butter, I can't tell you how much I love these cookies. I've run across many cookie recipes involving peanuts and peanut butter, and I have to say that these are the best. They are extremely rich and tasty and they are the simplest cookies to make in the history of cookie baking!

Ingredients
1 Cup Sugar
1 Cup Peanut Butter
1 Egg

Preparation:

Begin by preheating the oven to 350°F. Now mix together the egg, sugar and peanut butter. When you have the dough blended, pinch off small balls about a Tablespoon large, and drop them onto a greased cookie sheet about two inches apart.

Once you have the cookie sheet full of balls, take a fork and dip it into a glass of water and mash the balls down gently with the fork creating small lines. Then mash them down gently again in the other direction, creating a # pattern on each cookie. You will need to dip the fork in the water after every cookie to keep the fork from sticking. Bake for about 8-10 minutes and enjoy! This recipe is very easy to double or even triple.

Peanut Butter Fudge

Again, I love peanut butter and this fudge is a peanut butter lover's dream come true!

Ingredients
1 1/8 Cups Peanut Butter
2 Cups Marshmallow Cream
1 Teaspoon Vanilla Extract
¾ Cup Evaporated Milk
2 Cups Sugar
2 Tablespoons Butter

Preparation:
In a saucepan, begin by combining the evaporated milk, sugar and butter, then heating it until it comes to a rolling boil. Let the mixture boil for about 5 minutes, then remove it from the heat and add in the marshmallows, vanilla, and the peanut butter. Blend well and then spread the mixture into a greased 8 X 8 pan. Let the fudge cool and harden for several hours and then cut into squares and serve.

Candy Pie

This pie is extremely easy to prepare and is a favorite of my family. It's quick to make, and your guests will gobble it up even quicker!

Ingredients
1 Ready to Use Chocolate Crumb Pie Crust
1 1/2 Cups Milk
2 Packages Chocolate Instant
   Pudding Mix (3.9 each)
1 Tub Whipped Cream (Cool-Whip®) – 8 oz.
10 Small Bars of Chocolate
   Covered Graham Crackers
4-6 Additional Bars of Chocolate
   Covered Graham Crackers

Preparation:

Beat together the milk with the pudding mix and then add in half of the whipped cream. Beat together until completely blended and thick. Now, break up the 10 pieces of chocolate covered graham crackers into quartered pieces and fold them into the pudding mixture. Now, spread the mixture evenly onto the pie crust.

Next, spread the remaining whipped cream over the pudding mixture. Top with the remaining 6 crackers in a design of your choosing and refrigerate until chilled. You can crush the candy or cut them up and sprinkle.

Festive Menus

Winter Solstice
Yule Nog
Cranberry Snowballs
Shepherd's Pie
Caramel Apple Pecan Pie

Candlemas
Warm Apple Toddy
Chestnut Delights
Jambalaya
Peach Delight

Spring Equinox
Skyclad Punch
Walnut Treasures
Garlic Butter Spaghetti
Divine Cheesecake Lemon Bars

Beltane
Bitchin' Beltane Brew
Fruit Cream Pie Dip
Avocado Wraps
No Bake Blueberry Squares

Summer Solstice
White Witch
Eight Blessings Dip
Sweet Summer Solstice Chops
Coffee Can Ice Cream

Lughnassad
Witches Brew Ha
Hekate's Gift
Meatballs Deluxe with Spaghetti
Best Ever Lemon Pie

Fall Equinox
Caramel Apple Cider
Fall Fruit Dip
Hamburger Stew
Home-style Banana Pudding

Samhain
Spiced Cider Wine
Asgard's Spread
Chicken Casserole
Chocolate Pudding Cake

Moon Festivities

Because Full Moon festivities are more frequent, they tend to be less formal. Appetizers, drinks, and desserts would be fine for these events.

January
Amaretto hot Tea
Walnut Rounds
Winter Moon Compote

February
Black Magic Brew
Spicy Ham Tortilla Roll-ups
Nutty Chocolate Drops

March
Broom Burner Cider
Dill Cream Dreams
Chocolate Pudding Pie

April
Bananas & Berries
Spicy Berry Bread
Pink Cream Salad

May
Crème de Menthe
Barbeque Mini Links
Luscious Lemon Delights

June
Southern Sweet Tea
Jalapeno Hamburger Dip
Peanut Butter Ice Cream

July
Fuzzy Lemons
Ham & Pickle Roll-ups
Candy Pie

August
The Apple Goddess
Poseidon's Dip
Amazing Banana Sorbet

September
Runaway Broomstick
Green God Nibblers
Peanut Butter Cookies

October
Kitchen Witch's Absinthe
Tangy Bacon Swirls
Peanut Butter Fudge

November
Celtic Coffee
Nordic Dip
Scrumptious S'mores

December
Chocolate Mint Hot Toddy
Blue Brie
Chewy Choco Logs

Food Conversions & Equivalents Charts

Weights	
1 oz.	28 grams
2 oz.	55 grams
3 oz.	85 grams
4 oz.	115 grams
8 oz.	225 grams
16 oz.	455 grams

Food Measurements	
1/4 tsp.	1 ml.
1/2 tsp.	2 ml.
1 tsp.	5 ml.
1 tbsp.	15 ml.
1/4 cup	50 ml.
1/3 cup	75 ml.
1/2 cup	125 ml.
2/3 cup	150 ml.
3/4 cup	175 ml.
1 cup	250 ml.
1 pint	500 ml.
1 quart	1 liter

Equivalents

1 1/2 tsp.	1/2 tbsp.	1/4 oz.	7 grams
3 tsp.	1 tbsp.	1/2 oz.	14 grams
2 tbsp.	1/8 cup	1 oz.	28 grams
4 tbsp.	1/4 cup	2 oz.	55 grams
8 tbsp.	1/2 cup	4 oz.	115 grams
16 tbsp.	1 cup	8 oz.	225 grams

Liquid Equivalents

2 cups	1 pint	1/2 quart
4 cups	2 pints	1 quart
4 pints	2 quarts	1/2 gallon
8 pints	4 quarts	1 gallon

Liquid Measurements

1/2 fl. oz.	15 ml.	1 tbsp.
1 fl. oz.	30 ml.	1/8 cup
2 fl. oz.	60 ml.	1/4 cup
4 fl. oz.	120 ml.	1/2 cup
8 fl. oz	240 ml.	1 cup
16 fl. oz.	480 ml.	1 pint

About Dawn Flowers

Author, Dawn Flowers, is an East Texas writer, born and raised under the shade of the Piney Woods where she resides with her family and pets. She released her first book in 2001 and has since authored and published over thirty books on a wide range of subjects, including both fiction and non-fiction works, under a variety of pen names.

Her non-fiction titles reflect her love of religions, while her non-fiction titles reflect her love of horror. Most noted for her non-fiction metaphysical titles, she's also written and compiled twelve children's books for kids of the Christian, Jewish, and Wiccan faiths. Seven of her works were written and compiled under the name of Dawn Nefer-Aten, and were published for a non-profit, live-action, role-playing group, Amtgard, during her citizenship within the Kingdom of the Wetlands.

Her first fiction project, a short story titled, *In the Forest*, appeared in an eponymously titled collaborative book project with four other East Texas writers in 2011. The story was later revised into a horror novella. She then went on to write a series of six horror stories for children, with several more in the works.

Her most notable non-fiction works include *The Book of Dark & Light Shadows* and *The Spell Book of Wiccan Shadows*. Both titles were released online in 2011, and both rose to reach Amazon's #1 Best Seller rank for their categories, including Mysticism, Witchcraft, Paganism, and Neo Paganism. Almost a decade later, both titles continue to teeter within Amazon's top 100 best-selling books within their categories. For a complete list of available titles, bulk offers, or to keep up with new releases, you may visit DawnaFlowers.com, or follow her Facebook Page: Dawna Flowers Books.

An Original Publication of
UNDER THE MOON BOOKS

Copyright © 2004, Dawna Bowman Flowers

Pictures & Drawings Copyright © 2004, ClipArt.com

The font used throughout this book is Times New Roman

No part of this book may be reproduced without written permission from the publisher. Permissions may be obtained by contacting Dawna Bowman: dawnabowman@hotmail.com

Made in the USA
Monee, IL
18 September 2023